Clever Ratty

Written by Jenny Feely

Illustrated by Ian Forss

Flying Start
to Literacy®

T0342925

Contents

Chapter 1

What's hiding in the corner?   4

Chapter 2

A new member of the family   8

Chapter 3

Tell me a story   12

Chapter 4

The training begins   17

Chapter 5

The parade   23

Chapter 6

Ratty to the rescue!   29

A note from the author   32

Chapter 1

What's hiding in the corner?

"What's the matter, Joey?" Kara asks her little brother. He stands pressed against the kitchen wall, his eyes wide with fear. He opens his mouth to answer, but no words come out.

"Shall I get Mum?" Kara thinks that something terrible has happened.

Joey raises a shaky hand and points towards the far corner, beside the refrigerator. Kara can't see what her little brother is pointing at.

"Is it a spider?" she asks.

She hopes it isn't a spider because the only person more terrified of spiders than Joey is Kara.

"N-n-no." Joey's voice trembles. Kara realises that he is not far from tears.

Breathing quickly, Kara takes a small step towards the corner. Then one more small step. She peers into the dim corner between the refrigerator and the wall. She can't see anything, nothing has moved.

"There's nothing there, Joey," she declares. Suddenly, she spots something move, a flash of something brown with patches of white.

Whatever the thing is, thinks Kara, it's not a spider. It's bigger than a spider. Much, much bigger.

Once, Kara had watched her mother use a small towel to capture a terrified, hurt bird that had flown into a window. Mum explained that covering the bird helped to calm it down so they could take it to the vet. Kara thinks she could try to remove the "thing" in the corner the same way. She grabs a dish towel and moves closer.

"Oh!" she says. Her eyes widen. The thing is not a spider or a bird. "Joey, it's a little mouse!"

Joey yelps. If there is one thing that Joey is scared of, it is a mouse. No one knew why, but the sight of a mouse, even on a TV screen, would send Joey diving under a blanket, unable to look.

Kara reassures him. "It won't hurt you, Joey." But Joey could only yelp again.

Kara crouches to get a better view of the mouse. She can see the tremors of fear rippling across its body and up close she can also see that the scared little animal is not, in fact, a mouse.

"Don't worry, Joey," she says, as she raises the towel in both hands. "It's not a mouse – it's a rat!"

Suddenly, Joey comes to life, yelling "Aaagh!" and bolting out of the kitchen. Kara quickly covers the rat with the towel and picks it up in her arms.

"You poor thing," she croons, holding the quivering animal close. "Did Joey frighten you?"

Kara lifts a corner of the towel to peek at the rat. It seems calmer now, as it nestles in her hand. She removes the towel and the rat sits up on its haunches, craning its neck towards Kara, sniffing.

Kara begins to wonder. There is something odd about this situation, she thinks, something odd about this rat. A wild rat wouldn't sit and wait to get caught, when every instinct it had would be to make a run for it.

"You're not a wild rat, are you?" she says.

"It's all right," she adds, softly. "I won't hurt you."

The rat shivers a little, but Kara thinks its eyes seem less scared of her now. She positions her other hand, palm upwards, near the rat. The rat relaxes, dropping on all fours and dabbing at Kara's hand with its soft, cold nose.

It sniffs carefully and then it lifts its paws and creeps across Kara's hands.

As gently as a curling feather, Kara cups her hands around the rat and whispers, "You're safe now."

Chapter 2

A new member of the family

"He seems very used to being around people," says Mum. "We should put up posters to see if he belongs to someone."

Kara takes a photo of the rat and uses it on posters that she displays all over the neighbourhood. She knows that trying to find the rat's owner is the right thing to do, but in her heart of hearts she hopes that no one responds to the posters and that she can keep him.

"Since I don't know your name," Kara tells the rat, "I will call you Ratty."

Ratty seems to approve of his new name, as he sits on his back legs and washes his whiskers, a little grin on his face.

Ratty makes himself at home in a cage in Kara's bedroom.

A week goes by, then two, and Kara and Ratty become very good friends. She spends every minute that she can with Ratty. She takes Ratty for walks in the park, she watches TV with him and she even does her homework with Ratty perched on her lap. She looks after Ratty very well – every morning and night she makes sure that his cage is clean and that he always has fresh water and food.

When no one comes to claim Ratty, Kara is glad, because she would have been very sad to say goodbye to her new friend Ratty.

Mum makes friends with Ratty too, saving little pieces of food for him and letting him eat from her hand. Ratty always washes his whiskers before he takes the food.

"What excellent manners you have, Ratty," Mum laughs. "You even wash your hands and face before your dinner!"

Ratty wins Grandma over, too. On nice, sunny days, Grandma likes to sit outside with Ratty on her lap, gently stroking him, a faraway look on her face.

But, Joey does not make friends with Ratty.

Whenever he sees Ratty, his eyes fill with fear. Joey does not touch Ratty. He won't even stay in the same room as Ratty.

"This can't go on," Mum tells Kara. "This is Joey's home and he should feel comfortable and safe."

Kara's eyes fill with tears. She knows what Mum is suggesting. If Joey and Ratty don't become friends, Ratty will have to go.

"Don't worry, Kara," says Mum. "We will all help Joey to get along with Ratty, but if, in the end, he is still as upset as he is now, well ..." Her voice drifts off.

Chapter 3

Tell me a story

Kara tries everything she can to encourage Joey to stop being frightened of Ratty.

"He's really soft and gentle," insists Kara, as Ratty sits up on his hind legs, looking up at Joey. "And look at him! He wants to make friends with you."

Ratty sniffs at Joey who rears back, as if Ratty had zapped him with lightning, and runs out of the room.

"Ratty really is a dear little creature," Mum tells Joey. "He would never do anything to hurt you." Joey shrugs his shoulders and walks away.

For a long time, Grandma doesn't say or do anything to help Joey learn to like Ratty. She observes Joey and thinks a lot about how to help. Then, one day, she makes up her mind to tell Joey something she thinks will surprise him.

"Your grandpa would love Ratty," she says. Joey frowns. "Did you know that, during the war, Grandpa had a pet like Ratty?"

Joey looks hard at Grandma. Joey had only been four years old when Grandpa died, but he often picked up the framed photo of Grandpa and asked Grandma about him. What was he like? What did he do?

"I never met Grandpa's rat," Grandma goes on, "but I feel like he is a dear old friend to all of our family." Grandma lowers her voice and leans in. "In fact, without that clever, clever rat none of us would be here now."

Joey moves closer to Grandma and sits by her side. "Why?" he asks, wide-eyed. "What happened, Grandma?"

"It happened during the war," Grandma explains. "One day, Grandpa was digging a trench and he broke through the walls of a small burrow. Inside was the most terrified little animal – a rat. Grandpa quickly stepped aside to let the rat escape but it didn't run away. It looked up at Grandpa. He offered the rat some crumbs of food and, from then on, the rat lived in Grandpa's pack, keeping him company when he was on duty."

Joey doesn't notice that when Kara curls up next to Grandma, Ratty is in her pocket. He is far too interested in Grandma's story.

"Grandpa noticed that when a bomb was coming, the rat would squeak loudly. Your grandpa learnt to listen for this squeak and take cover. And that rat saved his life once."

"How could a rat do that?" Joey asks. He doesn't notice that Ratty has crawled out of Kara's pocket onto Grandma's lap.

"One night, Grandpa had set up his tent under a big oak tree. When he let the rat out of his pack, it ran out of the tent. It kept squeaking and squeaking, and wouldn't go back inside."

"In the end, to keep the peace, your grandpa moved his tent to the other side of the camp. And a good thing he did, too. During the night a huge branch fell off the big tree and set off a small bomb that was buried under the ground. That rat saved your grandpa's life!"

Grandma looks at Kara and Joey. "Without that rat, you two wouldn't be here."

Slowly, Grandma lifts her hand and begins to stroke Ratty. Kara glances at Joey and holds her breath, waiting to see what Joey will do. At first, catching sight of Ratty, Joey tenses a little, but gradually, he begins to relax. This gives Kara hope that Joey and Ratty could be friends one day and she decides to work even harder to make that happen.

Chapter 4

The training begins

After listening to Grandma's story, Kara decides to find out as much as she can about rats. She reads lots of information and discovers some surprising facts. Rats have an amazing sense of smell that is much better than people's. They also have very good hearing and they feel things with their whiskers. And some rats have been trained to do remarkable things. When Kara reads that some rats could even find bombs buried under the ground, she begins to think that the story about Grandpa's amazing rat must be true.

Kara has an idea. An idea that might make Joey view Ratty in a different way.

"Ratty," she says, "you and I are going to become treasure hunters. And Joey is going to help."

Kara plans a training schedule. Every day, Kara trains Ratty to find treasure.

At first, this training is simple. Kara places three small objects in Ratty's cage – a plastic button, a glass marble and a metal coin.

"Find the metal object, Ratty," says Kara. Ratty sniffs the three objects. When he goes to the coin, she gives him a little piece of banana to eat.

When he sniffs at the button or the marble, there is no banana for Ratty. Kara says, "Try again. Find the metal object."

Day after day, Kara trains Ratty and, in no time at all, Ratty knows to go straight to the metal object and sit down.

"Clever Ratty," Kara says, and picks him up and gives him two pieces of banana.

Then, it's time to do the next part of the training. Kara hides the objects under small boxes so that Ratty can't see them.

"Find the metal object," Kara says to Ratty.

Very soon, Ratty learns to sniff all the boxes and sit next to the one with the metal object under it.

He gets it right every time. And every time Kara gives him some banana.

"It's time to move on to the next part of your training," Kara says to Ratty. "Let's try this in the yard. And let's get Joey to help."

"I need your help to train Ratty to find treasure," Kara tells Joey, who shudders. "Don't worry, you don't have to touch Ratty. It's a treasure hunt."

"What do I have to do?" he asks, brightening. Joey loves treasure hunts.

"I will take Ratty into the house while you hide these treasures in the yard." She gives Joey four metal objects to hide – a coin, a piece of tinfoil, an earring and a safety pin.

"Not much of a treasure," Kara hears Joey mutter, as she takes Ratty inside.

After he hides the objects, he yells, "It's ready!" and disappears around the side of the house. From this position, he is far enough away from Ratty, but still able to keep an eye on the treasure hunt.

Kara isn't sure that Ratty will be able to find all four hidden objects because the yard is so big. She encourages Ratty.

"You can do it," she says. "Find the metal objects, Ratty."

At first, Ratty looks confused. Then his whiskers began to twitch. Soon he is sniffing his way all around the yard. He sniffs a stone, but keeps going. He sniffs a leaf, but keeps going. Then he sniffs a piece of tinfoil and sits down.

"Clever Ratty!" Kara smiles and gives him a piece of banana. Soon, Ratty finds the other metal objects that Joey has hidden.

Kara and Ratty practise the treasure hunts every day, until Kara is certain that Ratty can find any metal object, anywhere in the yard. And every time, Joey helps by hiding the objects. Some days, he stays in the yard to watch Ratty searching and, sometimes, he grins when Ratty finds an object that he had hidden in a very difficult spot. Kara always encourages Joey to offer Ratty a piece of banana, but he resists, every single time.

Then, one day, something happens that changes Joey's mind about Ratty.

Chapter 5

The parade

Every year, in the town where Kara lives, lots of people march in a big parade to remember the people who had been to war. Kara's family had always cheered as Grandpa marched past, his shiny medals proudly displayed on his chest. Grandma always had a smile on her face and a tear in her eye.

But, this year is different. For the first time, Grandpa isn't there to march and everyone, especially Grandma, is very sad.

"Joey and Kara can wear the medals," says Grandma. "They can march in place of Grandpa."

"Oh, I'm not sure about that," says Mum. "It's a big responsibility."

"It *is* a big responsibility," agrees Grandma, "but your father would be so proud to have his grandchildren wear his medals."

"What if something happens to the medals?" asks Mum.

"Joey and Kara will take care of them," says Grandma.

On the morning of the parade, Joey is excited to be marching for Grandpa, but his mood changes when Kara pops Ratty in her pocket.

"Rats can't come to the parade," he says.

"Why not?" Kara argues. "Grandpa's rat was a hero. Grandpa would like that Ratty is marching, too."

"I don't think it's right to take Ratty," says Joey. "People will think you are making fun of the parade."

Kara doesn't know what to say. Perhaps Joey is right, she thinks. Sadly, she places Ratty back in his cage.

"I'll bring you a treat from the picnic afterwards," she promises.

Before the parade starts, Grandma opens the old velvet box that contains Grandpa's medals.

"Be very careful with these medals," Grandma tells Kara and Joey, as she pins the medals on their clothes. "These are Grandpa's medals and they are precious to me."

Joey and Kara march proudly from the town hall and
down the main street. A band plays and people line the
street to clap, as they walk past.

At the end of the march, people gather at the park for a picnic. Joey climbs trees with his friend Charlie and Kara plays with her friends. Mum shakes out the picnic blanket and spreads it on the grass. Mum and Grandma set out the food and Joey and Kara rush over to join them. They are very hungry after the excitement of the parade.

As Grandma passes a sandwich to Joey, she gasps. "Where is Grandpa's medal?" she asks, pointing at his chest. There is a small rip in the shirt where she had pinned the medal.

Joey's face drops. "Oh, no!" he cries. "It must be here somewhere, Grandma. I had it when I got to the park. I showed it to Charlie. Then we went climbing in the big oak tree. I must have lost it there."

They search and search on the ground under the big oak tree, looking under leaves and in nearby bushes, but they can't find the medal.

"We'll never find it now," says Grandma, gloomily. "I'm afraid it's gone for good."

"Wait," says Joey. "I have an idea."

He turns to Kara, his mouth set in a determined line. "Get Ratty!"

Chapter 6

Ratty to the rescue

Kara places Ratty on the ground under the tree.

"Find the metal object," she commands.

Ratty sniffs all around the bottom of the tree. He pokes his nose under leaves and into cracks in the roots of the tree. Around and around the tree he goes. He does not find anything made of metal.

"It's no good," Kara says. "The medal is not here."

Joey doesn't say anything. He fears that Grandpa's medal is lost for good.

"It's getting dark," says Mum. "Let's go home."

Kara reaches to pick up Ratty, but he jumps away from her grasp and begins to sniff at the tree trunk.

"What is it, Ratty?" Kara asks. "What have you found?"

Ratty keeps sniffing. Then his whiskers begin to twitch. Ratty climbs up the tree. Up and up and up, until at last he stops and sits very still next to a small hole in the trunk of the tree.

"He's found something!" Kara shouts.

Joey is already climbing the tree. Up and up and up to where Ratty sits. He reaches into the hole and feels around. Then, with a joyous whoop, Joey pulls out his hand, his fist clenched around an object.

"I've got it!" he yells. "I've got Grandpa's medal!"

Joey picks up Ratty and holds him close. Then he carefully puts Ratty into his pocket and climbs down the tree.

Safely on the ground, he hands the medal back to Grandma. "I'm sorry, Grandma."

Joey looks at Kara. "Thanks," he says, giving his sister a big smile.

"You should thank Ratty," she replies.

"Thank you, clever Ratty," says Joey. "You can come home with me now."

A note from the author

I'm very interested in learning about those things that animals can do that people can't. How do animals do it? How do rats smell things that I can't? How can they use their whiskers to sense their surroundings?

It amazes me and makes me think about whether people are cleverer than animals. Then I learnt about HeroRATs and I realised that maybe the cleverest things happen when animals and humans work together. This gave me the idea for this story.